AF278446

poxo

poems by

Isaac Chavarria

Slough Press   College Station

Copyright © 2013

All rights reserved.

For orders and information:
Slough Press
3009 Normand
College Station, Texas 77845
sloughpress@gmail.com

Acknowledgements:

"Boom Town" first published in Rio Grande Review online, Fall 2007/Spring 2008

"Six colonia words," "Jarrón," and "ode to lover" first published in The Acentos Review, (online), December 2008

Cover Art by Beatriz Guzman Velasquez

Book Design by Christopher Carmona

Author Photo by Ladislao Martinez

Library of Congress Control Number: 2013945720

ISBN-10: 0941720187

ISBN-13: 978-0-941720-18-2

Special Thanks:

to all who encouraged me to write when i didn't believe in myself, gracias. para los que se encuentran en mi poesía, perdóname. for those who have entered my life and left, i'll see you later. emmy pérez, for expecting more and the countless opportunities. dr. steven schneider, you taught me form and now i can break it. most of all to diana, who has lived and supported me through many of these words.

Dedication:

To my mother, Maria de Jesus Chavarría, te amo.

Introduction

My poetry collection began as an exploration of my identity, which usually referred to Hispanic. I was told Chicano was a better choice, and even though I understood the significance of the term, I rejected it and eventually found the term pocho. Scholarly and literary works define pocho as an Americanized Mexican, focusing on the inability to speak proficient Spanish. Furthermore, the portrayals highlight not knowing enough of the Mexican culture and not fitting in as an American.

As the term Chican@ gained popularity, the discussion of pocho tapered off and I thought, did the pocho disappear? Recent research shows the pocho still exists, but is an overlooked character and identity. And in response I write and hope pocho is not simply defined by language, but also by strengths and flaws.

It is said that Mexican Americans exist between the worlds of the American y el Mexicano. Pero, el pocho is also between two worlds: Hispanic y Chican@. After living a lifetime as a pocho, I feel confident in my identity. Now I can say I am a particular type of pocho of Mexican descent, living along the border, and learning how to live in a hometown where we love and hate each other for who we are. soy poxo.

Table of Contents

DESARRAIGADOS

BARRIO-COLONIA

MEXCLADO

DESARRAIGADOS

en enero

el clima dice
calienta el tlalpeño
y saca las cobijas

in January

a cool front suggests
reheat the tlalpeño soup
and take down blankets

igualito

i can't remember your eyes;
brown i believe.
but i recall Strawberry
and the 92-win Mets on TV—
exhales—
falling asleep shirtless

on Sundays after mass in San Martín
your curses tearing at a motionless Chevy
sending tubing and sparkplugs
into my stomach

rushing through
beady Budweiser's
cooled by a churning
window unit
7 lost seasons later

La familia-
menos tú
se amontona
cradled by unkept huizache branches
near oil stains
where your Chevy died.

¿a dónde se fueron
tus golpes y maldiciones

que prefirieron saborear
semillas de mesquite
y plantar sin maceta?

tu silencio
tal vez
encontró a otro hijo

and whispers
{mamá, vero, Jr, yvonne}

¿Recuerdas a papá?

He's just like papá.

mamá

pienso tanto en ti
y los desayunos rasquaches

{un huevo,
cuchara de frijoles,
repollo para ensalada,
y postre de jícama}

pienso tanto en ti
que nunca digo cuando me voy

{noches por la ventana
pasando casas quemadas
a lujuria y lago}

nunca digo cuando me voy
para que no te preocupes

{si dios quiere nos vemos
este fin
de semana}

si un día no regreso,
tampoco debes preocuparte.

---

mom

i miss you
and impromptu breakfasts

{an egg,
spoonful of beans,
a shredded cabbage salad,
and jícama for dessert}

i miss you so much
i don't tell you when i leave

{nights through the window
passing burned houses
to lust and a lake}

i never tell you i am gone
so you will not worry

{god willing
i will see you this weekend}

if one day i don't come back
you shouldn't worry

construction

a trowel	sliding	bottles
my father's	on grit	cutting
palette	sealing	grey hair
smothering	a tomb	encased
cement	choking	in cheap
and plaster	on broken	amber

víboras

on dad's
heat-driven
madness days

jr. and i
squatted
in a hollow
pond

we strung
garter snakes
pierced on
mesquite twigs

waiting for
our mother's
resurfacing

canciones de la casa

my dad, after carpentry jobs,
drank a few beers
sat on faux La-Z-Boy.
my mother sat on a chair next to him
also with a beer

in silence a

now near midnight
i call my mother
¿Le gustaba música a mi papá?

her yes is quick
but stumbles on specifics
¿Marisela?
maybe, but he loved romanticas

No sé qué decidiste
pero yo firme estoy
 y a tu amor no voy a renunciar
i thought he was more macho.

¿Avía algo que no le gustaba?
his disappointment of us
scarred my mother
but she didn't remember him
disliking one cantante
over another.

She said he liked canciones regionales
y los del rio.
I don't know what either means.

maybe my mother
preferred silence
and he, after arguments
with his father
listened to politico radio,

and returned home to mix
random beatings
with romance.

lechuzas

después de una
noche de mano
a mano
me miras
escuchando
las líneas azules
en mi mente
reconociendo
mis pasos

cunado encuentras
mi mano entre
sus dedos
las garras
escarban mi piel

hasta en la obscuridad
reconoces mis pasos
y a veces
creo que te mirare
en mi camino

en la cama
me quitas paz
me sigues
escuchando
y en fin

cuando estoy solo
apareces ojos
negros y verdes

a medianoche
tus gritos
eres viejo casado
y yo te digo
eres lechuza

spirit to bird

when you find
our hands intertwined
your claws
dig my skin

in darkness
my steps are familiar
to you

in bed you take
away my peace
listening

until i am alone
during a supermoon
your screams
you're a married
prick.
i tell you
you are a lechuza.

mi abuelita

I.
is a cliché driven monster
filling her snake
and chicken quota

in between cuentos
of the ranchito,
sweeping dirt floors con palmas
selling cliché chiclets
con los niños en Las Cumbres, Reynosa, Tamaulipas, México
struggling to forget
random spousal beatings

abuelita is
sixty five years
of brown river floods

II.
when we buy tortillas
hecho a máquina y plastic
my grandmother is like yours

wrinkled, uncared for, unskilled
holding her respirator
talking about snakes
icon
of the ranchito
lost in the state
of Aguascalientes, México

III.
Our grandmother
talks about
clipping mesquite
seeds
sucking sweet
green
to pass time.

she crossed
el rio bravo
and came back

our grandmother was
taken care of by her
son and grandson in Rio Grande City

she died
a machine consuming
the last scent
of ranchito.

regresando from the midwest

lately, my mother retells the same stories. her favorite is when she,
my dad, and our tío and tía were returning from Iowa. each time the
story is told for a different reason. this time she's telling me because
my 17 year old brother is about to buy a car del año. she's telling us of
the long trip coming down con Jr., Yvonne, y Vero recién nacida in the
truck my dad bought for $200 dollars. my dad heard a thumping noise
and asked my mom to check the tire while he drove a little bit to see
where the noise was coming from. Imaginate, he asked my mom
and not my tío. pues, she did, and es que las tuercas no estaban bien
puestas en una de las llantas. reflecting, at the moment, my mom says
lo bueno es que lo encontramos between the hidden context of male
dominance
migrant story, cross
cultural story, she
narrows it
down to
tuercas
en una
llanta
chueca.

entero

la Mexicana pobre
 y el Americano rico
se encontraron en la frontera

se abrazan
y de ahí
 nací yo

 criado por la tierra
libre de los Estados y
 la maternidad de México

pero soy más que Mexicano
 más que Americano
 soy Tejano
 Hispano
 una mezcla de culturas
 buscando un nombre

bl ank

vida: leaning on a pole
rusted y cansado
en la pulga, after the cross
through Anzaldúa's subdued

blank

on the curb of salvation
army, me pides una peseta
¿de dónde eres?
    de allá. te doy la peseta.

blank

fishing man
this side of the Americas
gathering his Talapias
and swimming back home

blank

from mildew park benches
avoiding blue patrol lights
sleeping in the dragging
night

blank

i see you.
uprooted and implanted
far from *allá*
arid and bare pescados.

el río

There are río bravo orphans
greeting us with battered palms
breaking through a rebar fence

among palpations of bridge crossers
hearts of children, women, no men
watched by la migra in *no persons* land

one day an orphan is thin, aged, and pregnant
months later she is calling, begging
ne-kuls for her newborn, para su hija

begging from shoppers walking across
and over como gigantes
pounding the rust into their lives

we call them natives on the río grande
we call ourselves migrants
pero somos huérfanos del río

un poco de you

when you went to Donna ISD, they barred all the chiquillos en kinder
from speaking Spanish but los activistas won and there was no more
punishment for speaking with one more tongue. now you teach
your daughters more English so they can fit in where 90% of us are
brown(ish). You want tus niños to fit in, like you didn't [it wasn't just
about the paddle when you spoke Spanish; it was about being labeled
Mexican-uneducated-una chiquilla mocosa y estúpida]. and los malos
have won because tu hija can speak Spanish at school now, but when
she speaks, it's crooked, unlike everybody else's. and now she dislikes
those who speak Spanish because she feels alienated. they allow
Spanish, but now it's for people who just crossed over. it means you
haven't been here long enough.

so who won?

los malos made Spanish into a course,
  [about who you'll never be]
developed French
  [funded and exotic]
because football is the American way
  [not futbol]
and Texas is crazy about turning you

into a güerita
you taught your daughters well
to lay a thick foundation
on their cheeks
cover lunares
and how to avoid shame

Americanized Boy

Juega con tu chalupa
   R.C jeep
     toys

Toys que blinka
 g.i.-toys, toys
  don't worry
they grows
from the donation
of some time
get three
tienes money?
 five

your toys
esta tan fine
  tus jugetes
quiero steal
   your toys

loaded

melissa lies
plump
caressing
her motherhood
stifled and hot
thighs cold
against block walls
melissa waits
for resurrection

on a mattress
drunk passion
gasps for romance
and relishes
a familiarity
of burning
the body
a single bedroom
apartment
melissa's plump
child savoring
chocolate dripping
on his belly

la llorona

cuando tuve 17 años
tuve un niño,
que lo amaba. pero lo
más difícil era no
estar con él solamente
los fin de semanas
hasta cuando año
por año el fin era
un día y después
dos semanas, y mi
ex me dijo que
quería child support.
Pues ella pensó que
me iba dejar, pero
quería mi hijo más
fuimos al corte
y me dieron
un paternity test.
Me dijo lo que
me imaginaba.
No era el padre.
Después de eso
decidí que era
mejor no vivir
una mentira
y ahora tengo un dolor
que nunca se me va.
siempre espero escuchar su voz
tal vez pasar por el en la tienda
me falta ese amor
de mi hijo
de una familia
y a mi esposa
siempre le pregunto
hijos
donde está
mi hijo

crying woman

at 17 years
i had a kid
i loved
but lived
without
on weekdays
each year
a day
became two
weeks
until my ex
wanted child support.
she thought i
wouldn't protest
but we went
to court and
i got test
results saying
i know sacrifice
does not color
brown skin
güero.
i decided no more
and i'm left
with pain to catch
his voice, pass him
i am missing
that love
of my son—
mi familia—
and to my wife
i ask
hijos
where is
my son?

archetype abuela stories

de pelos sueltos
always en la casa
para cuidar
her children,
y los niños de sus niños

who won't look
at mom's eyes
the ojos
of abuelo posing
con la otra mujer.

i do not ask
if grandmothers
are immaculate

cuando una le quita
el cheque
a su hija

otra grita
a niños brincando
en la sofá de plastic
¡bájate! ¡ bájate!
¿Quieres que te arregle?

abuelita disowns a son
for marrying a Mexicana,
like she once was

a harvester
whose husband
enjoyed being Johnny Appleseed
con mujeres de la patria

estas historias
in the name of 'buelitas
para no recordar abuelos

en las palabras de mi mamá

nomas con que vives honestamente
she told my brother
porque cuando haces algo
contra la ley
no se siente bien

yo me recuerdo cuando
tu papá y yo estuvimos
sin papeles

Pues, tuvimos papeles
Pero eran de la notaria.

Y a ese tiempo estaban
diciendo que ya no.

Y cada vez que miraba
la inmigración
she turns her hands
in a churning motion
over her stomach

le decía a tu papá
recuerdaté la escuela
a dónde van los niños
y los grados, y a que
horas salen

so that when he crossed
over and back
he could prove
he lived here.

en la vida después

mi madre
me da abrazos
y mis lágrimas
regresan en nubes
cúmulos
regando coronas
de cristo

pero aquí no hay
subtítulos y muchos
hijos regresan
después de
despidos eternos-
por amantes

tus puñetazos
fallan
a corregirme
y tus defectos
son olvidados

p o r q u é

aquí
la vida
es un lazo
sobre mi
cuello.

---

in the afterlife

my mother hugs
me into tears
feeding flowers
of a corona
de cristo

but here i don't have
subtitles or translations
and sons return
after lovers
don't want amor

from beatings
failing to fix
me and defects
are forgotten

why because?

life here
is a memory

BARRIO-COLONIA

path

canal along the street
hidden by trees and never speaks
road for travesuras unseen

in another life

colonia trees
are tagged
landmarks

engraved

by extranjeros
tongue-fed whispers
to second lovers

they aren't dishonored
or confused
among peers
about identity:

standing to exist,
shelter,
and cry meaning

en Alton

middle America's
auburn street
slopes
into 5 mile line

drywall casas
wading in
WIC
liquor
pawn
shop

Esquina Mart's
individual
10¢ cigarettes

for kids
through canal
pathways

sifting
bottles shattered
fences

and into
Main Street
America

encontré

ramienta, buganvilias
piratas y cojidas

busco de todo
que es taboo

la virgen y la santísima
los sobadores
la idioma de la patria
ilegales, trabajadores, padres

ven a mirar
lo que te falta

rusted tonka trucks
películas gay
vicios entre plátanos y papayas
vendido en la forma
de mi papa con la otra

i found

tools, red flowers,
pirates, and gimps

searching for taboo

a virgin and her
death sister,
body healers,
a native tongue
illegals, workers, fathers

come see
what your missing

tonka trucks rusted
gay films
vice by the pound
sold in the form
of my father
with his mistress.

safety

lo que necesito es
cruzarme-
reassurance
the sky is not falling
and I'm ascending
to heaven
a familiar colonia,
parvo dogs,
and paint scrawled walls

un cielo
where comfort
es un tipo de barrio-colonia love
tus amores con mis celos
gritos sin golpes

un colonia love
que apenas cruzo
y duerme
en caliche y colchones

y mi barrio love
is up for grabs.
tag it
or break into it,
give it a fist fight
for expression.

Pero mi comfort –
like my love –
resembles
mobile home lies
creeping into niños
watching su padre
in a crazy carro
doing doughnuts
screaming caliche
and paternity test.

`memorias: some i would rather forget`

a. my sister, hands up, between my mom and dad. In the air, his hands, el sartén.

b. no snow for more than a century. That night i spun out, and totaled a car.

c. opening an old suitcase to find *Playboys* my brother left behind, gone.

d. coming home to find my basketball cards & cd's stolen.

e. stolen: TV, $100 in coins, and my bottle of *Presidente*. After call, Sheriff arrives hours later.

f. walking colonia canals, pumping bb gun, and aiming at Budweiser bottles.

g. looking at photo and realizing i've been getting browner over the years.

h. stealing my father's money and how revenge felt, until i realized i didn't get the worst of it.

i. my mom says, *nomas con que estés feliz y haces tus pagos.*

j. about to take a mid-term herpetology exam in grad school and quitting on the spot.

5 Reasons

a child is broken
when a father
says, I don't know
my own strength.
I want you
to shut up.
Can you smell
the liquor, purging
from my body?
I wish you
never existed
but this will be
our little secret.

un mix de historia

i met caperucita roja
con sus tasty
pásteles, a clean
cut niña
going to abuela's house.

esa niña roja
unaware of a dancing
devil en el baile,
hoof steps waking
borrachos.

y la lechuza,
perched on a huizache
screeching at love
making silhouettes.

cuidado, little red
riding hood.
do not dance
with the handsome stranger
do not steal
your neighbor's husband.

six colonia words

When I say brown,
think of rhythmic flows
filling these colonia
houses on the hill, like birds
in smoke from a blunt when she puffs
when I say I see

boundaries, intertwined by a river to the sea
that goes within my eyes, low and brown
filling her puffs
of pale rocks/dark fisherman flows
by drowning birds
filling this colonia

she rides on torn sheets from colonia
dumpsters. sounds from a sea
of screaming, begging birds
like the pounding of his brown
fist through air flows
pinching her puffs.

my friend does puffs.
she says a night on the colonia
lets us feel the flows
the catfish would feel if in the sea
of brown inside brown
all the way down to the birds

black birds, grey birds, just birds
all from one's puffs
of cotton turned into brown
spots of water on colonia
dirt roads changing to a sea
where kids put plywood bits to flow

using the same word flows
the air gives to mockingbirds
and sounds to my sea

making me dream of puffs
in my trailer home colonia
to this charco of brown
forms miniature seas seeping below rigid flows of dirt
into brown potting soil for pajaritos on tripping wires
to feast as they puff & climb down along colonia air

no me escondo

instead of the backyard
en el cuartito
i'm igual
que los vecinos
fajitas y pollo en la parilla
proud on the front porch
y otros put a hammock on the elm
la vecina washes a VW
y le sube al volumen hasta cuando
se oiga lo mínimo de tres casas

Ramón Ayala canta
para poder llegar a ti
es todo tan difícil

vivir aquí
los maleas comiéndose
la calle y la policía
con golpes
por mujer

es difícil cunado roban
los regalos
mientras festejas

nos hacemos
perros guardianes

we become less of a back-
yard gente.
despertando con cada rumbo
de gritos

saturday night
parties de conjunto
con el sonido de los bukis
entre mis piernas

i don't hide

under the back porch
and instead i take center
stage like the neighbors,
chicken and fajitas grilling,
a hammock on the elm,
and neighbors vw blasting
ramón ayala a minimum
of three houses down

singing *it's so difficult*
to get to you

here the badasses
consume the street
and the police
with fist
for a woman

it's difficult, robbed
of Christmas gifts
while celebrating

we become guard dogs
and less of a back-
yard raza
waking with each rumble
of screams

at saturday night
cojunto parties
los bukis sound
between my legs

mientras los caminos
atrás de la casa
son caminos
de los colores
de bandidos
escolares que dicen
una persona es gastada
en libros de inquietud
aunque los colores nos siguen
hasta enterrarlos en tus campos.
tus colores dicen lo que escuchamos
entre nuestro pecho

while canal pathways
full of color
of scholarly bandits
preaching a life
is wasted on books
of unease
even though colors
follow us to death
and listen.

Fiesta para dos

The neighbors cook out
and feed the dogs, bones
give them a sensation
of being human
the way we
walk towards each
other – we step
we dance
follow the chairs,
empty seats,
and admire
a dragonfly
from a nymph
una chica
a quinceañera
and we share a cup –
151 rum con mentiras
of where we once were

there was almost an incident
when the small pickup truck
was a gust of dirt and force
and the gritos
pushed us indoors
there was almost a time I fell
out of love
a place
where I worked my bones
into words
filling my mouth
like lips.

Copas

visitando el vecino
es como narco-corridos
y tequila
lenguas del origen
mixtiado
con el futuro
de mi madre
pasado

past
of my mother
with the future
mixed
barrio-colonia tongues
and tequila
is narco-corridos
visiting the neighbor

Drinks

Fruiting

let's divide
our bodies
into juxtaposing

sounds
of chicharra
evenings
and tap water
on toes

your watermelon
taste on my skin
your grapefruit peels
stinging

like pots and pans
rhythm

Jarrón

by fire
is burned
brown

water jarrón
blue streaks
dipped from tin
can

jarrón de abuela
on golden grass
decorating
two tone dirt

shaded brown
southwest girls
make un jarrón
for cactus

Reynosa I

hace quince años
caminaba con mis padres
en el centro

ellos fueron
a comprar queso
y aguacate

y yo fui
a chispas
para jugar
arcade games

antes cuando
simplemente
era un diversión
y yo no era
americano,
ni poxo
o chicano

cuando yo
era una niño
me gustaba
caminar entre
el centro
inadvertido

Reynosa II

In my grandfather's house
mamá was in the kitchen
dad in abuelo's room.

They talked
como coyotes enojados
and all i could catch
from his berrinche was
no, es que

y estos días digo
después de odiarlo

no, es que

    los ricos no entienden

no, es que

    no nos dejan

no, es que

    nos mienten

no, es que

    siempre seremos pobres

no, es que

    ella está enojada

no, es que

    no es lo mismo

no, es que

en los estados unidos es diferente

no, es que

ya no es mi hijo

no, es que

somos hechos de vicios

no, es que

no sé qué decir

Summer

Heat changes people.
We become brown,
darker than what we are.

And angry –
not souls,
just from the burn.

On our backs
we are imprinted
by our clothes
our burdens.

We are summer people.
We live here
in the heat.

Boom Town

from father's porch
and city
on the grow, providing workers
services, anything
for the goal, the entity, that first
class ride to upper lower
class, from the poverty
WIC lines and grabbing of
indigenous alien
cracker barrel philosophy
linen towels
picking the thorn
and throwing it back to the bush
so that more dirt than pavement
street of shoeless children
and pamper tax break
stops being a way of life
so terrible enough to inspire
a bottle of cheap Puerto Rican rum
mixed with thrift store cola.

Citrus Parade

on the edge
of border
creationism, children
bailan Tlacolorerosis.
and i am
myth
beaten by the sun
and a dog chain.

my mother overheard
two güeros saying,
Been to Progreso?
It's like not a damn Mexican there
knows how to finish concrete

and I stood
watching Mission High ROTC
march
hands clapping
pride and eyes
of Missouri
loving every frame of
cheerleaders
citrus
festival
cold.

toxic rain only in alton

I know it was wrong
stealing your intimate object
but I'll ask my sister
to give back your husband.

once you get him,
tell me a story
about a stem cell
dividing into two
then more pairs
breaking up into tissues and organs
monitoring themselves –
check and balance
deciding what we think and how it's done.
because we don't have credentials,
money wrapped in pockets
of city cop looking for a bust

according to the news
everything is in alton
even 24 miles from here, it happens in alton.

tell me why a grackle falls silent
when the lawn is wet
a bird's comic timing
of teardrop eyes closing
to target practice
bottles breaking on canal depths
spreading glass diatoms
into water burning from lead
faded into manmade ponds
drying in the summer.

lead-drops on barrio-colonia species
tacuaches hiding under a trailer home
Kantunil y Linares streets
the entirety of esposos
y salvavidas

watching as a blond
lifts breaks up waves
of café
acid wash on my skin.

In alton también

viejitos
like jóvenes
caminan despacito
a sus casitas

and their viejas
  [y la mía]
jumping over
chorizo oil

we [used to]
go to mass
at san martín de porres
singing away confessions
on top of hail mary's

  [we do]
dance into sin
en la pulga

shifting between
expired merchandise
and damaged goods:

a plastic horse missing a leg
  Jorge con su cojera
Barbie, minus su ropa
  y Rita, too dark

for a good lay

sylvia vela park

is for gorditos
caminando
cada dia
la güera con su hijo
kids that come over
if you stand with
a basketball
they wait
for the rebound
like alley cats
do you choo them away
or let them take up
your time?

it's even for wannabe
lovebirds
scribbling
names,
never into eternity

soccer kids
softball tots

rip up
splinters

dive onto their
bellyful of rocks

three hundred
sixty five
days

y los viejitos
todavía se conocen
aquí, escondidos
con una sancha.

les platican del
parque, que en
la noche se convierte
en la isla del padre.

y los niños corren
a gusto.
déjelos que se cansen
para que duerman
tranquilos.

para que mi dedos
acaricien tus
vicios.

Esas dos millas

the census says
my town is 4,306 dots
of pobreza
4 mile line to 6 mile line,
one mile east to west.

¿y que de mi cuñado?
a citizen –
after the census –
but still
and the priest in
San Martín de Porres
listen, kneels, prays
for more than 4 thousand.

poor Catholics go to San Martín,
even ones who live closer to
our Lady of Guadalupe, porque
aquí you can get un desayuno
of two tacos for $1
American.

past 6 mile line,
girls like Inez, still attended
Alton Elementary, even if she didn't
live in Alton.

your pencil
lines are boundaries
my boundary es la calle
del taco –
la esquina donde ese señor
vende sandías
  [sin semillas]
and the pavement
leads to caliche

boundaries for all of us,

because passing la pulga
we are in the census,
checked, evaluated,
scratched off.

don't count this Martinez
ese Hernandez

and for my niece, esa panadería,
la Esquina Mart, esas dos millas
they are the world to her.
y así es para mí.

Querida Valle

– after Rigo Tovar

en este lado de la frontera
brincamos para la cumbia,
banda, internacional, techno

en la pulga de San Juan
con las señoras maduras
vigilando las jóvenes

y no nos vamos
hasta que ahogamos
las penas

hasta cuando la banda
anima que agarren
su última bebida
y baile.

querida amor
siempre regresaré
y bailaré un huapango
querida valle

Dear Valley

– after Rigo Tovar

on this side of the border
we jump in cumbias,
banda, international, and techno

at the San Juan flea market
with the mature ladies
eyeing their chicks

we don't leave
until we drown
our shame

until the band
urges us to grab
our last bud
and babe

my love
i will always come back
and dance a huapango,
dear valley

MEXCLADO

borracho

under the influence of poxo
the güero said
give me some car
nita tacos, so
da mexicana
and a papa
to go.

New Orleans street jazz

under drizzle, makes me tear
`hearing tu llanto.

Lucent

The lights flashed out
I daydreamed about
sinister alley ways
sprouting from
fields of oranges
of life
machismo
rising dawn
at twilight's tips.

I dreamt
of the valiente
a stench of overnight Presidente
purging from his body.

I wanted freedom

from my mother's
seven day work week
cleaning homes
because she's better than that –
to some
I wanted freedom,
like my dad,
fajazos beating my mom,
slipping out a locked door

and I wonder
if some days my father
cries out of frustration –
as I do –
to be understood.

lotería familiar

el prieto
se va al norte

la Yvonne
tiene el pelo chino
como papá

la Vero
ojos que desaparecen
con su sonría

el flaco
con su carabina
y las hurracas

la quieta
le corta el cabello
al payasito

el bebe
sigue creciendo
hasta cuando se valla.

No le pares hablando a la familia.
¿Quien tiene estos dos?
¿A quien le falta el prieto?
¿Agregamos a la ninis?
Vamos a quitar ese.
Cada año unos cambios
de cuadros para la
lotería familiar.

Mexican Family Lottery

the dark skinned son
leaves north

la yvonne
has curly hair
like her estranged father

la vero
eyes disappear
with her smile

the skinny son
with his bb gun
and grackles

the quiet one
cuts her clowns
hair

the baby
grows until he leaves

Don't stop communication
Who has these two?
Who's missing the dark skinned son?
We add "la ninis"?
Let's remove this one.
Each year we change
the cards
of the family bingo

Para mi family

I am *poxo*,
a MeChiCan of America
raised in the valley.
My father a carpenter
my mom cleaning homes
Mexican rich, American poor.

angry poor
on being called *poxo*
respond, *Chale homes*
least I'm no hippie child America
styling carpenter
jeans in a Cali valley.

Lots of poor in the *valle*.
colonia poor
homes eaten by carpenter
ants, pincher on a *poxo*
looking for the America
of luxury in homes

is foreign to homes
in the colonia. At times I forget the *valle*
is on this side of *América*.
Regardless, I still feel poor
and being called *poxo*
is as bad as carpenter.

Jesus was a *carpintero*
and so was Jesús hanging with his *homes*
drinking Budweiser, far from *poxo*
nights en la soledad de la *valle*
waiting for the poor
of *América*

The same land of *Américo*
Paredes, being built by a *carpintero*
who is just *pobre*

no *homes*
isolated in a floodplain *valle*
como otro *poxo*

Some parents came poor to America,
hungry, rewarded by poxo children ashamed of carpenters
unaware of being *homes* in the Valley

ode to lover

you speak
 texts
short quips
 of ambience

you taste
 a smoky scent
absorb peace
 in passing

 make blood
rush warm
 summer
river

like canal
 through fruit
field

channeling
 to red
flowers

Dial-a-Curandera

Dial-a-curandera
on the radio
remedies
on your spouse
powder
on his pillow
for eternal,
unbreakable
love, a humming
bird wrapped
in red string.

dial on
the radio
because her
blue house
chips
are now ashes
smothered

esa curandera

cúrame del malo
    burdening mi corazón
cúrame de borrachadas
que defina cada fin
de semana
y gritos frightening dogs
into alarma

place a red cloth
sobre mi cuerpo
  read the dark
lines of my life
  y cura
la manera de mi amor.

dame poder
to deflect gritos
de puto e infiel

dame poder
to forgive myself
cúrame de este amor
que casi me deja.

comezón

has me
cruzando los pies
like un hijo
de dios
pidiendo perdón

que comezón
en mis piernas
en el ombligo
even my own
corazón
dice basta!

sí –
i don't deny it –
el cuerpo rechaza
el desconocido
igual que el corazón
dice
no seas callada
don't look away
no te vayas

consume mi
piel café
my sangre
de mex
i is yo
can es puede

entre
dedos
on our hands
heart
en nuestro cuerpo

déjame
sin este comezón
corazón

In the fields

I take lovers
to bite on lushness –
a sweet-sour mist
at ripeness

gasps and loves
flashback

to Richard's
run, go, run
with stolen citrus

and torn stems
clinging
            a bitter fear
the mud
to my escape

i park
grasping now
sweet-sour
plush

crashing.
the slit
of a window
urging me.

Listening

within vowels
desperate
clings of throwback
nights
drip on the back
of my cheek
and speak as
they travel down
creating goose bumps
and hunger pains

the sounds
climb over each other
toppling to fit
into your partially
open mouth

Bilingual

If you speak to me in Spanish, why
do I care for you more? Why do
your words explode sentiment?
Because of the possibilities,
because of shared experiences? Am I
foolish to love your Spanish, to read
those texts yet translated? Do I
love your language whether it's scholarly
or colloquial? Does it matter if you
are from Nicaragua, always speaking inglés
with an accent? Does it matter that traditions
don't have to die?

ode to chaparras

a pudgy mix of cubana,
india, y americana
a stout statuette

on the faults of the frontera
above las palmas
que nos dice

hello
please leave: don't come back

goodbye
welcome: you are home

mi statue de contradicción
como su hermana
en Nueva York

a bridge
for the trickle
near Anzaldúa's park-
true bareness
makes it easy
to spot transients

succession

it's like the baby comes first
then maybe if you're a good
baby's momma I'll hand you
a ring so you can show it
off to your family, and your
father always wants to play
the lottery so he has me
pick his numbers cuz he thinks
I'm lucky I don't ever marry
you because I'm just like those
stupid kids. I fuck before I know
fuck before I say Mary, Mary
Marry me, so I know you're mine.
marry me because I can't take
the way my father punches my mother.
mary, oh my friends are gone
into that abandoned house
and I want to follow them.
they like to feed themselves
to whitewall canvas.
they feed themselves
to hands on caliche.
and I say, oh mary
mary, madre mia.

hijo de tu

pachuco padre,
holding up paredes
con el pie derecho
the tip of his cigarrillo,
breaking a fog

es un vato
mandando su hijo
a la chingada,
the land of
brown bag lunches.

only hijos de pachucos
cross through Housing,
and blessings de la Virgen,
pasando familias
depositing faith
into their marinito

échale ganas
*   pon atención*
para que salgas adelante

little piggy
a bit light-skinned
and rose-cheeked
en su uniform
colored with traces
de pachuco
y poxo.

Sangre

de mi padre,
sangre que tal vez
es un poco de moreno
porque mi padre–
chino–
tiene ganchos
negros
que lastiman.

tengo sangre de machista
y infiel. la raza
de mi tío
asesinado por tener amante
olvidado por la ley
y sus hijos.

matrimonio
promesas
pelo corto
no pueden parar patillas
que se me enchinan

y los glóbulos de rojo,
blanco, y verde
es una mezcla
de corajudo,
silencio, y
deseo
peligroso.

Blood

of my father
perhaps a bit
dark because his hair
curled into hooks
which injure

i have chauvinist
and unfaithful blood
la raza of my uncle
assassinated, forgotten
by the law
and his sons
for having a lover

marriage
promises
cut hair
cannot stop my curling
sideburns

and the cells of red,
white, and green
is a mix
of quick temper,
silence, and dangerous
desire.

roots

When cutting
south texas
huizache,
a tar-
covered stump
eliminates
buried, hacked
and chopped ancestors
from returning as
hungry offshoots

las cruces

wooden markers
grounded in
caliche y coronas
de cristo

cruces
dwindling as i
move north. Cruces para
Fernando y Micaela Torres

pero las cruces para ti
de Saúl
    están escondidas
y Gabriel,
    entre las yerbas

no se miran,
o tal vez nunca existieron.

en recuerdo
i didn't go
to your funeral
i didn't mourn
and sometimes i still expect to run into you
picking up some barbacoa en Jr's.

y no tengo una cruz
pero sí tengo lágrimas
that we won't ever
ride our bikes into the pond
of photos, snakes, y sunsets

y no tengo cruz
pero sí hay
gritos para ti

No se terminan

a border wall
aplastando la tierra
separating you from me
me from them

a border patrol station
in Falfurrias
every trip we answer
"Yes, sir" to
Are you a U.S citizen?
Alton, Mission, Rio Grande Valley
las tierras desgraciadas, to
Where are you coming from?
"Yes, sir" to
Is this your car?

don't deport me
like you did that stranger
years ago –
yesterday.
don't pull me over
like you do
mi hermano,
prieto.

a border's mentality
in San Anton
dismissing
Tlatilco fertility
statuettes and
some half
brown skinned
tourist.

Un wetback en San Antonio

Un wetback en San Antonio
me preguntó, *¿me tomas una foto?*
I search my vocabulary,
pero the easiest thing to say
es que *sí.*
Le tomé la foto con su
Polaroid camera
so he could tell his story
to someone, who turned out
to be su mujer
que lo está esperando en algún
rancho de México.
Nos dijo de su vieja
y que caminó desde el valle
a San Antonio.
I laugh inside
but I think that's how
the journey felt.
He's lucky to have found
some work in
las cocinas en San Antonio.
He's just wanting his family
to know how he is:
una Polaroid
en el parque.

even if I haven't been there

if I visit east la I want to survive ese chicano/a culture. I grew up in
south [don't call me Mexican-fresa-American-gringo] Texas.
I am afraid of my synchronizada turning into a giant burrito. I don't
want to run into a día de los muertos parade without anyone to
mourn. I don't want to be asked where my parents are from, nomás
para decir *un ranchito*.
I want to teach them about botanas and the art of chip, cheese, bean,
fajita, chicken, quesadilla placement. I want to teach them that a fresa
is not just a fruit.

Streetcars

are the safest way to get around in New Orleans.
They move slowly enough so you can talk
yourself into a romantic image. but when
walking, when walking, you feel vulnerable
like the gutted buildings. you notice the homeless
don't have anywhere to go. The sign says
the park is closed for renovation,
but they do it to keep out the homeless.
Depending on the time,
you may feel at home, when tourists
travel by streetcar during midday.
or at night, when the immigrants
viajan, los que todavía tienen acento.

Lookers

is the type of place ten
dollars will buy your
waitress a drink.
what she does with
the drink is up to her
but before the drink
she walks with you
to the dance floor
baila cerca, cerca,
but not close enough
for you to notice her
belly, maybe pregnant.
go to Lookers
find the new trend
in immigration. Small
cantinas where construction
workers sit on fold-out
tables. They wear comfortable
clothes because the only
women are the waitresses.
They go to drink, play
pool, and to be with
someone like themselves.

Sounds

If we come for exotic jazz, then
what do we do when we walk into
the ghetto, looking for alcohol in a can,
running into morenos on their
porch steps, mother loud-talking
to their children. Is this the
jazz, a broken beat of trumpets
sitting outside convenience store,
eyeing me stranger? or cajun accordions
wheezing their first breath.

tomate

¿y qué? when güeros become folk stories
or equate to 5%, when I see las lomas de Rio Grande
y no sé quién es culpable. Desde la isla, los caliches en Alton,
McAllen clubs, brown no se conoce because you got prietos,
bolillos, cafecitos, tanned y todos
odian uno al otro porque unos parecen muy nacos
otros fresas, es como una ensalada where cherry
tomatoes envy the fall aesthetic of heirloom tomatoes
in turn, heirlooms think Beefsteak tomatoes are sellouts
cuz they are in hamburgers, pizzas, pretty much anything

regardless vienen del labor
darker each year,
but never enough to be wild
como el que nomás no me cae,
who says his ancestors are Aztec, where his name was *xitomatl*
but now its *tomati.*

cafe

brown has been all around, each day each year, tomorrow. brown when i opened my eyes to the brick fence. brown farther out on rooftops and inside the bus, brown bobbing on potholes. brown all around means it is difficult to be a mecha chicano. it means you are fighting against the brown around you. the brown you are a part of does not understand why boycotting mcdonalds is important because its pretty much the only thing we can afford. brown of the outside doesn't understand the anger. brown doesn't even understand why light brown call themselves chicanos. they could be mexicanos, latinos, hispanics, white, poxos, mochos. everyday it's brown. sometimes speck of white, black, in between shades. but always brown all around.

Salvavidas
en la alberca
 contando cabezas
  de cabello café, negro
café, negro, café

y vigilando esa
cabeza guerra
 como muñeca consumada
por café y negro

Lifeguard

In the swimming pool
counting heads
of brown hair, black
brown, black, tan

and trailing
that blond haired
doll consumed
by brown and black

conquistadora

she came like a conquistadora
all güera, full of border
notions and old
west spirit: cheap mezcal,
gun battles, and poverty.

plunges her fingers
into ruby red toronjas
a jumble
of morning dew
and pesticides

if bubaloo's
white *VLR 13* tee
is a collage of
cholos and clocks
don't think
he's a gangsta
he's just a pubescent
chicano in the making.

teach for
barrio–shaded kids

and believe
i teach for the Américas

post colonial malinches

- after pocha catalana's painting of the same name

say goodbye [and fuck you too]
father y fajazos.
padre enojado
porque ella se fue
and ingested educational
poison
in kaleidoscopic cells,

otras malinches del valle
son más quietas
and use a hummingbird
tied in a string
of red under
a lover's pillow

malinches son hijas –
traitors to la casa
y reglas
de un machismo
mutado

at funerals
ellas dig themselves
feet first into caliche,
4-chambered hearts adorning
a pale awkwardness

returning to la frontera
para ofrecer
su liberación
como testamento
de una malinche
moderna

un frontera poxo en san antonio

pregunta:

dónde está the no
license, fly by noche
taquerías, tex-mex buffet
piratas hawked by
chicas en
mini-faldas.

y

mom?
still paranoid
nunca se queda
sentada
quier hacer
to-
do

o

como encuentro
el chisme de un paletero
corn en un vaso
y midnight
raspas?

Respuesta:

¿Quién sabe?
But stop by
la alameda and market
square.
Tal vez encuentras
cacahuate japonés,
un gansito de chocolate
photos of Mexican
placas
pero aplácate

con las morenitas

and during lunch
in Milam Park
cierra tus ojos
y será como Reynosa,
español sin acentos
los carros alrededor
gritando tu nombre.

Un Poxo en San Antonio's "First Friday"

lo que no tenemos siempre se parece
más. y lo que no cay es más pesado.
pero no miramos la manera
que los cocineros
sus niños con la abuela
hasta la 1.
que piensa esto es una fiesta
de música y bebidas
pero esto es fiesta
de customers
preguntando por especiales
que no se van hasta
la 1. Fiesta donde
a wrong turn
grabs the attention
of police.

i had a sueño

en mi sueño
jay leno
was on my old 19'
black and white
curtains to say
buenas noches

pero i preferred
topo gigio
que me ponga
a la camita
con su rat dance.

y en vez de
la little mermaid
wanting to take me
under the sea,
con su acento Mexicana
el ratón vaquero dice
*What the heck is this house
for a manly Cowboy Mouse?*

i had a dream

in my dream
jay leno
was on my old 19'
black and white
curtains to say
good night

but I preferred
topo gigio
to put me to bed
with his rat dance.

and instead of the little
mermaid wanting to take
me under the sea,
the cowboy mouse
with a Mexican accent
says *What the heck is this house
for a manly Cowboy Mouse?*

even chicanos

get asco
at a prieto
complexion
and light siblings
even chicanos

visit poxo-
land-
and don't come back

even chicanos

hide behind
jesus, maiden
names, and peacocks

even chicanos

chug budweiser
screaming mother
¿por qué no me visitas?

even chicanos

marry güeritas
own an only child
and live complacently
ever after

Another year, una pregunta más

Aren't I an oxy-
stereotype,
un childless
chicano?

it's not just
the marriage clock
counting the months

soy yo
contando las ramas
del huizache

shading
el carro, sobrinos,
ese gato vagabundo

que una noche
con su gata
me burla

contemplating

cultural icons
under a microscope

juan camaney
  [sexist or blue-collar]

switch

 edward james olmos
   [pioneer or mexicano stereotype]

switch

raúl salinas
  [cell mate or poet]

switch

selena
  [idol or adultress]

switch

Alton, TX
  [barrio-colonia or dumping ground]

switch
Las Cumbres, Reynosa, Tamaulipas, México
  [sister city or travel advisory]

switch

poxo
[identity o identidad]

switch

frontera

to border zone

switch

Poxo to
Chicano/a
to Hispanic
y back

switch

hasta cuando
I'm topsy turvy
y ni se donde
estoy or which
cultura i speak.

Being a non-believer and Mexican American means

[only] attending mass
in case of:
first born baptisms, quinceañeras
and emergency weddings.
It means a hundred pairs
of crossed fingers
in the name of

      the father
holy   and   spirit
     son

a non-believer
kneels and holds back
hands –
the repetition
amen, amen
a men y mujeres

curanderos—
power derived from dios—
are deaf and mute.

promesas—
in the name of el padre—
and in death.

for a non-believer
la Virgen de Guadalupe
will never appear

palm sunday
ash wednesday
good friday

to be godless
almost means
not being chicano

Poxo Questions

why can't I roll my r's when Andrea la güera can?
¿y por qué Tesalónica se convirtió en Tessy?
when did the pulga become ghetto?
what is the equivalent of bob in spanish?
were you always that brown?
how do i sound when i speak español?
quinceañeras, baptisms and weddings count as attending church?
how do you say "happy hour" in Spanish?
is it "homes" or "holmes"?
si me voy, can i come back?

soy poxo

como Américo Paredes
es el orgullo

como José Antonio Villarreal
lo escribió

como Richard Rodriguez
no lo quiere

como inmigrantes
se convierten

como usted
no entiende

como Juan Camaney
no es [pero yo quisiera que si]

como Selena y Los Dinos
lo canta

como Lalo Alcaraz
lo dibuja

yo soy poxo

i am poxo

like Américo Paredes
is the pride

like José Antonio Villarreal
wrote it

like Richard Rodríguez
does not want it

like immigrants
become

like you
don't understand

like Juan Camaney
is not [but i wish he was]

like Selena y Los Dinos
sang

like Lalo Alcaraz
draws it

i am poxo

BIOGRAPHICAL SKETCH

Isaac Chavarría earned a Bachelors of Science in Biology from the University of Texas-Pan American in 2001. He has previously worked at UTPA as a writing center tutor, biology lab assistant, and sports editor for *The Pan American*. His current degree is a Masters of Fine Arts in Creative Writing, awarded from The University of Texas-Pan American in 2010.
e-mail: tx.popper@gmail.com

CPSIA information can be obtained
at www.ICGtesting.com
Printed in the USA
LVHW021437070219
606759LV00001B/88/P